CLAUDETTE
COLVIN

DiscoverRoo
An Imprint of Pop!
popbooksonline.com

Martha London

abdobooks.com

Published by Pop!, a division of ABDO, PO Box 398166, Minneapolis, Minnesota 55439. Copyright © 2020 by POP, LLC. International copyrights reserved in all countries. No part of this book may be reproduced in any form without written permission from the publisher. Pop!™ is a trademark and logo of POP, LLC.

Printed in the United States of America, North Mankato, Minnesota

052019
092019

 THIS BOOK CONTAINS RECYCLED MATERIALS

Cover Photo: Archive PL/Alamy

Interior Photos: Archive PL/Alamy, 1; Julie Jacobson/AP Images, 5; Shutterstock Images, 6, 7, 9, 14, 23 (bottom), 30, 31; Everett Collection/Newscom, 8, 17; US National Archives and Records Administration, 11 (top), 22 (top), 25 (document); iStockphoto, 11 (bottom), 23 (top), 25 (gavel), 28; Horace Cort/AP Images, 12, 18; Red Line Editorial, 15; AP Images, 19, 26; Rex Wholster/Alamy, 20–21; Esther Bubley/Library of Congress, 22 (bottom); Basement Stock/Alamy, 27; Richard Harbus/Polaris/Newscom, 29

Editor: Brienna Rossiter
Series Designer: Sarah Taplin

Library of Congress Control Number: 2018964783

Publisher's Cataloging-in-Publication Data

Names: London, Martha, author.

Title: Claudette Colvin / by Martha London.

Description: Minneapolis, Minnesota : Pop!, 2020 | Series: Amazing young people | Includes online resources and index.

Identifiers: ISBN 9781532163654 (lib. bdg.) | ISBN 9781644940389 (pbk.) | ISBN 9781532165092 (ebook)

Subjects: LCSH: Colvin, Claudette, 1939- --Juvenile literature. | Civil rights activists--Biography--Juvenile literature. | Segregation in transportation--Juvenile literature. | Civil rights movements--United States--History--20th century--Juvenile literature.

Classification: DDC 323.092 [B]--dc23

WELCOME TO DiscoverRoo!

Pop open this book and you'll find QR codes loaded with information, so you can learn even more!

Scan this code* and others like it while you read, or visit the website below to make this book pop!

popbooksonline.com/claudette-colvin

*Scanning QR codes requires a web-enabled smart device with a QR code reader app and a camera.

TABLE OF CONTENTS

CHAPTER 1
ENDING SEGREGATION

Claudette Colvin grew up in Alabama.

She was part of the **civil rights movement**. This movement took place in the 1950s and 1960s. At the time, **segregation** was common in many

WATCH A VIDEO HERE!

Claudette Colvin played a key role in ending segregation on public buses.

states. Laws kept black people and white

people separate.

The laws said some stores and restaurants were for white people only. Black people were not allowed to go there. Also, black people could not sit in certain sections of buses or trains.

Segregation laws said black and white passengers had to use separate waiting rooms.

Boys stand outside a segregated theatre in Leland, Mississippi, in 1939.

They had to use separate bathrooms and

water fountains too.

DID YOU KNOW? Even libraries and movie theatres were segregated.

Some protesters sat at whites-only restaurants.

To **protest** these laws, some

people refused to follow them.

Claudette was one of the first people to challenge segregation on buses. Her brave actions helped bring an end to the unfair laws.

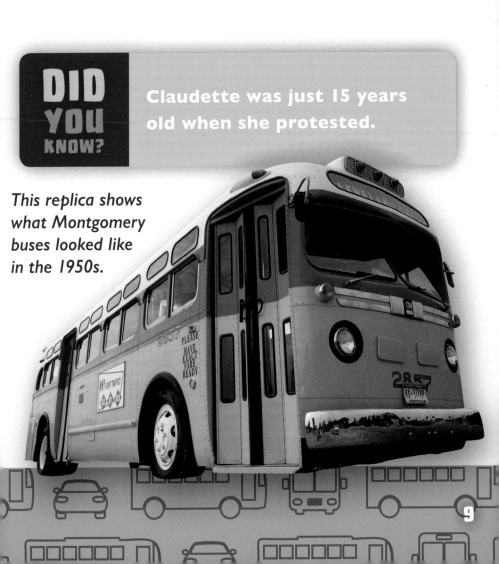

Claudette was just 15 years old when she protested.

This replica shows what Montgomery buses looked like in the 1950s.

CHAPTER 2
THE BUS RIDE

Claudette Colvin was born on

September 5, 1939. She lived in

Montgomery, Alabama. Like other black

children, Claudette went to an all-black

school. In 1954, **segregation** in schools

COMPLETE AN
ACTIVITY HERE!

First graders study at an all-black school in South Pittsburg, Tennessee, in 1948.

became illegal. But many states ignored

this law, especially in the South.

Schools for black students often had fewer books and supplies.

Passengers of other vehicles, such as this trolley, faced segregated seating too.

Claudette took a bus to and from school each day. Because of segregation, black people had to sit near the back of the bus. The front seats were for white people only. If the front seats filled up, black people had to give their seats to white passengers. If there were no more seats, black people had to stand.

DID YOU KNOW? Black people had to pay fines of up to 25 dollars if they didn't give up their seats.

On March 2, 1955, Claudette and three friends were on their way home. A white woman boarded the bus. There were no open seats. The bus driver told Claudette and her friends to move. Claudette's friends moved. But Claudette did not.

In 1955, a bus ticket cost 10 cents.

BUS SECTIONS

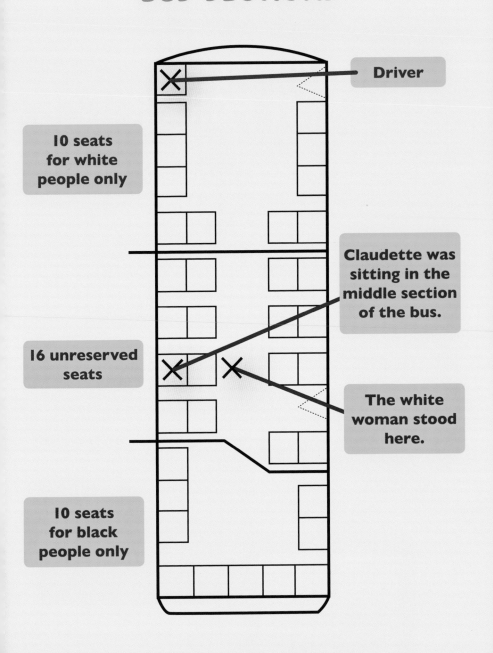

Driver

10 seats for white people only

Claudette was sitting in the middle section of the bus.

16 unreserved seats

The white woman stood here.

10 seats for black people only

Claudette refused to give up her seat.

So, she was arrested and taken to jail.

Nine months later, another black woman

refused to give a white person her seat.

Her name was Rosa Parks. She lived in

LEARN MORE HERE!

A police officer fingerprints Rosa Parks after her arrest in December 1955.

Montgomery too. Like Claudette, she

was sent to jail.

An empty bus drives down a street in Montgomery during the boycott.

This time, the black community

took action. They decided to **boycott**

DID YOU KNOW? To help the boycott, some taxi drivers charged lower fees.

Georgia Gilmore supported the boycott by providing food for the protesters.

the bus company. Black people refused to ride segregated buses until the law changed.

MONTGOMERY BUS BOYCOTT

The bus boycott lasted 13 months. During this time, many people walked or shared their cars. Some people rode in taxis. By refusing to ride buses, the protesters caused the bus company to lose money. They hoped this would convince the city to change its rules.

Meanwhile, a lawyer sued the city

of Montgomery. He said **segregation**

laws went against black people's rights.

The case was first heard at the US District Court in Montgomery.

Claudette **testified** at the trial. So did

three other women who had refused to

give up their seats.

TIMELINE

SEPTEMBER 5, 1939
Claudette Colvin is born in
Montgomery, Alabama.

MARCH 2, 1955
Claudette refuses to give up
her seat on a bus to a white
woman.

DECEMBER 1, 1955

Rosa Parks is arrested for refusing to give up her seat.

NOVEMBER 13, 1956

The US Supreme Court rules that bus segregation is unconstitutional.

DECEMBER 5, 1955

The Montgomery Bus Boycott begins.

DECEMBER 20, 1956

The Montgomery Bus Boycott ends.

CHAPTER 4
HIDDEN HERO

The case against bus segregation went all the way to the US Supreme Court. This is the highest court in the United States. On November 13, 1956, the court announced its decision.

LEARN MORE HERE!

The case was known as **Browder v. Gayle.**

IN THE DISTRICT COURT OF THE UNITED STATES

FOR THE MIDDLE DISTRICT OF ALABAMA

NORTHERN DIVISION

FILED

JUN 19 1956

D. C. DOBSON
Clerk

By _____ Deputy Clerk

AURELIA S. BROWDER, and
SUSIE McDONALD and CLAUDETTE
COLVIN, by Q. P. Colvin, next
friend, and MARY LOUISE SMITH,
by Frank Smith, next friend,
and others similarly situated,

Plaintiffs,

vs.

NO. 1147

W. A. GAYLE, CLYDE SELLERS and
FRANK PARKS, individually and
as members of the Board of
Commissioners of the City of
Montgomery, Alabama, and
GOODWYN J. RUPPENTHAL, individually
and as Chief of Police of the City
of Montgomery, Alabama, and
THE MONTGOMERY CITY LINES, INC.,
a corporation, and JAMES F. BLAKE,
and ROBERT CLEERE, and C. C. (JACK)
OWEN, JIMMY HITCHCOCK, and SIBYL
POOL, as members of the ALABAMA
PUBLIC SERVICE COMMISSION,

Defendants.

JUDGMENT

This cause came on to be heard b

court duly convened pursuant to the provis

United States Code, Sections 2281 and 2284.

After trial on the merits and ca

of the evidence therein adduced and after or

submission of briefs by all parties, the Cou

advised in the premises, found in an op

June 5, 1956, that the enforce

passengers on motor buses

as required by Sect   and 31c) of

Code of A   , as amended, and Sectio

e Code of the City of Montgome

stitution and laws of the Un

After the Supreme Court's decision, black and white passengers sat together.

The court said **segregation** on buses was **unconstitutional**. That meant it went against the law. Because of this decision, segregation on buses became illegal in every US state.

Claudette played a key role in this important change. But for many years, few people knew she had been involved.

In some states, people used tokens to pay for public transportation.

Claudette moved to New York after high school. She didn't talk much about her past. In 2009, a book was written about her life. Since then, more people have learned about her important role in the **civil rights movement**.

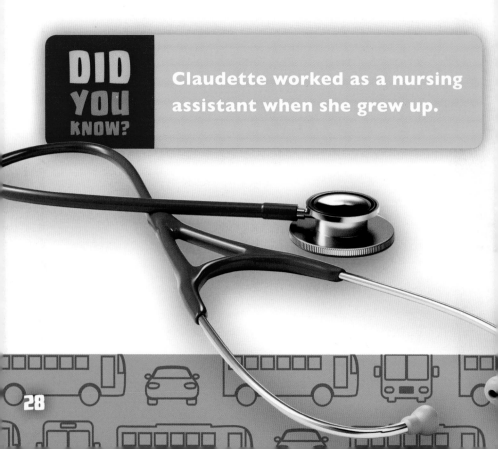

DID YOU KNOW?

Claudette worked as a nursing assistant when she grew up.

In recent years, Claudette has begun talking more about her past.

MAKING CONNECTIONS

TEXT-TO-SELF

Have you ever been treated differently because of how you look? How did that make you feel?

TEXT-TO-TEXT

Have you read another book about someone who was part of the civil rights movement? How was that person's life similar to Claudette's? How was it different?

TEXT-TO-WORLD

Segregation caused black people to be treated unequally. What are some ways specific groups of people are treated unfairly today?

GLOSSARY

boycott – to stop using or buying something until changes are made.

civil rights movement – a struggle in the 1950s and 1960s that involved people working to gain equal rights for black people.

protest – to use words or actions to show disagreement.

segregation – separating people based on the color of their skin.

testify – to tell a court about one's experience.

unconstitutional – going against the US Constitution, the document that contains basic US law and protects the rights of citizens.

INDEX

ONLINE RESOURCES

popbooksonline.com

Scan this code* and others like it while you read, or visit the website below to make this book pop!

popbooksonline.com/claudette-colvin

*Scanning QR codes requires a web-enabled smart device with a QR code reader app and a camera.